Hidden NEW JERSEY

Written by **Linda J. Barth**
Illustrated by **Hazel Mitchell**

Mackinac Island Press
for the love of reading

*Our gold dome gleams in the afternoon sun
and shows where a major battle was won.
Patriots' Week is loads of fun.
Meet Thomas Paine and Washington.*

John A. Roebling opened his wire-rope factory in Trenton and made cables for many suspension bridges and aqueducts. The Brooklyn Bridge is his company's most famous creation.

The state seal has three plows and a horse to remind us that farming is New Jersey's heritage. Liberty, carrying a liberty cap, and Ceres, holding a horn of plenty, stand on either side.

John A. Roebling

The Grounds for Sculpture, in Hamilton, feature 3-D versions of French Impressionist paintings! Stroll the grounds and have a picnic among these fascinating sculptures.

THE GREAT SEAL OF THE STATE OF NEW JERSEY

LIBERTY AND PROSP 1776

TREN

Search for...

Schooner

Vase

Wig

Teacup and saucer

Bill of Law

How beautifully the gold dome of the State House gleams in the sun. It is the third oldest capitol in the country. (Only Maryland's and Virginia's are older.)

In 1898 the first professional basketball game was played in Trenton.

While you're in the State House rotunda, look up to see the inside of the dome. Can you find the fire-breathing dragons under the staircase?

March on down to Trenton between Christmas and New Year's for Patriots' Week, honoring the Battle of Trenton. It is seven days of tours, talks, trials, concerts, reenactments, and just plain fun. Meet George Washington, Thomas Paine, and a host of other colonial folk.

Trenton falls—really only a rapids—marks the limit of navigation on the Delaware River. Since ships could go no farther north, Trenton became a busy port.

Visit the State House and play "Make a Law!" At the Welcome Center, experience Just Jersey, fun facts and trivia about the state. See how many you know!

"TRENTON MAKES—THE WORLD TAKES." These words (in gigantic neon letters on a bridge) remind us of the many products that were made here: vases, sinks, dishes, bathtubs, and wire rope cable (used to hold up suspension bridges).

The first New Jersey railroad, the Camden & Amboy, crossed the state in 1833. Its famous locomotive, the *John Bull*, is the oldest operating steam locomotive in the world. You can see it in the Smithsonian Museum of American History in Washington, DC.

Through the narrow waist you'll cross the Garden State. Ride the old John Bull and visit gardens most ornate!

Mules trotted on a towpath along the Delaware River and Raritan Canal, pulling boats across the narrow waist from Bordentown to New Brunswick.

The great scientist Albert Einstein lived and worked in Princeton for more than twenty years.

The first college football game was played along the bank of the Raritan River in 1869: Rutgers defeated Princeton, 6-4.

The College of New Jersey moved its students from Elizabeth to Princeton in 1756, later changing its name to Princeton University.

Search for...

Purple Heart

Red cardinal

Rutgers 'R'

Mule

Airmail plane

The "narrow waist" is the skinny middle of the state, the shortest distance between the Delaware and Hudson rivers.

Thomas Mundy Peterson

Albert Einstein

Gunnery Sgt. John Basilone

Woodrow Wilson

Woodrow Wilson served as president of Princeton University, governor of New Jersey, and president of the United States.

In 1870, in Perth Amboy, Thomas Mundy Peterson cast his ballot as the first black voter in the United States.

If you have a cut or scrape, thank Earle Dickson of Johnson & Johnson for inventing the Band-Aid® brand adhesive bandage in New Brunswick in 1920.

Raritan's hometown hero, Gunnery Sgt. John Basilone, was the only enlisted Marine in World War II to receive the Purple Heart, the Navy Cross and the Congressional Medal of Honor.

Duke Gardens was the home of millionaire James B. Duke, who created lakes, waterfalls, and gardens on his private estate in Hillsborough. The gardens are now open to the public for biking, walking, and bird-watching.

Stand on Washington Rock in Green Brook and look out over the valley, as General Washington did. Can you see the British troops marching across New Jersey?

During the American Revolution, George Washington and the Continental Army spent more time in New Jersey than in any other colony. That's why Congress named the state "The Crossroads of the American Revolution National Heritage Area."

George Washington's superb, that sly old fox.
Winning our independence, he really truly rocks!

Marching and fighting on dark days and bright,
they crossed the Delaware on a cold Christmas Night.
His army fought battles in towns and on plains,
they beat our British rivals by using their brains.

When the troops were camped in Morristown in 1777, Washington ordered everyone to be inoculated against smallpox, a dreaded illness. That "shot" saved many from getting this contagious, often fatal, disease.

Look on the back of the New Jersey state quarter to see the famous painting *Washington Crossing the Delaware.*

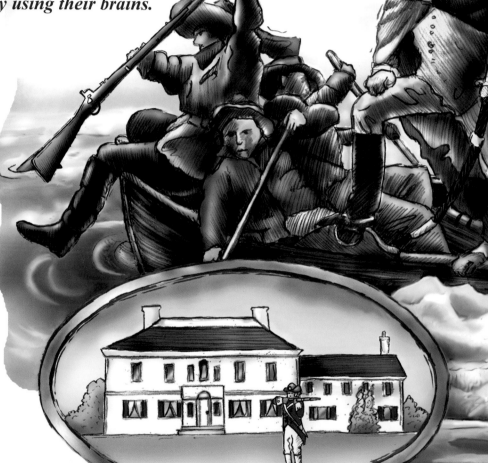

During the Battle of Monmouth in June 1778, the British and Continentals fought for hours in sweltering heat. Molly Hays, a woman who traveled with the army, brought water and ammunition to the soldiers. Later she became known as Molly Pitcher.

Search for...

Soldier

Shaving brush

State quarter

Cannon

Musket

The winter of 1779-1780 was so cold that the Hudson River froze solid! The British could take heavy cannon and horses across the ice, since it was 12 ft thick!

At Rockingham, near Princeton, examine exact replicas of Washington's uniform, his wooden shaving case, his leather portmanteau (trunk), and his folding bedstead.

Mary (Molly) Hays

George Washington

Surprise! On Christmas Night in 1776, General Washington sneaked his army across the Delaware River in Durham boats. They marched through the frigid, snowy night to Trenton to capture the Hessians at their barracks.

While camped at Jockey Hollow, the soldiers built more than one thousand log huts. Over twenty snowstorms kept supplies from reaching the camp. Still only a small percentage of the men died from starvation and cold.

In 1779 in Bridgewater, the Continental Army paraded in a grand review before five Indian chiefs. General Washington wanted to show the army's strength and win the Indians' support.

"George Washington Slept Here" is true of many towns in New Jersey. You can visit the headquarters of George and his generals in Somerville, Kingston, South Bound Brook, Bridgewater, and Wayne.

Seven lighthouses dot New Jersey's coast, once known as the graveyard of the Atlantic. Barnegat, Absecon, Sandy Hook, and Cape May are the tallest. Sea Girt and Hereford Inlet are quaint Victorian houses with short towers.

In New Jersey we love to go "down the shore"
for beaches and boating and, oh, so much more.
Our miles of coastline get all the raves
as we play in the sand and swim in the waves.

Inventor Guglielmo Marconi demonstrated the first commercial use of the wireless telegraph at Twin Lights on the Navesink Highlands. Located on the highest point on the East Coast, the station sent and received messages on a regular basis.

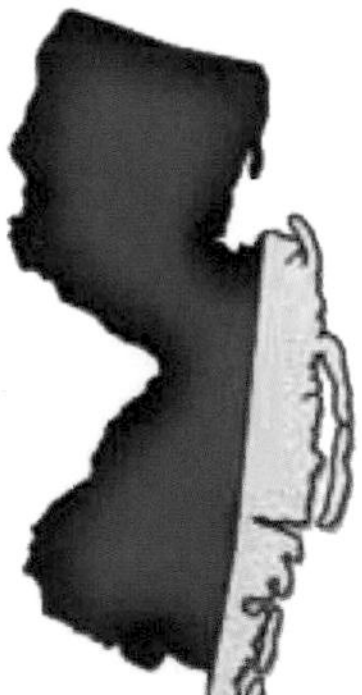

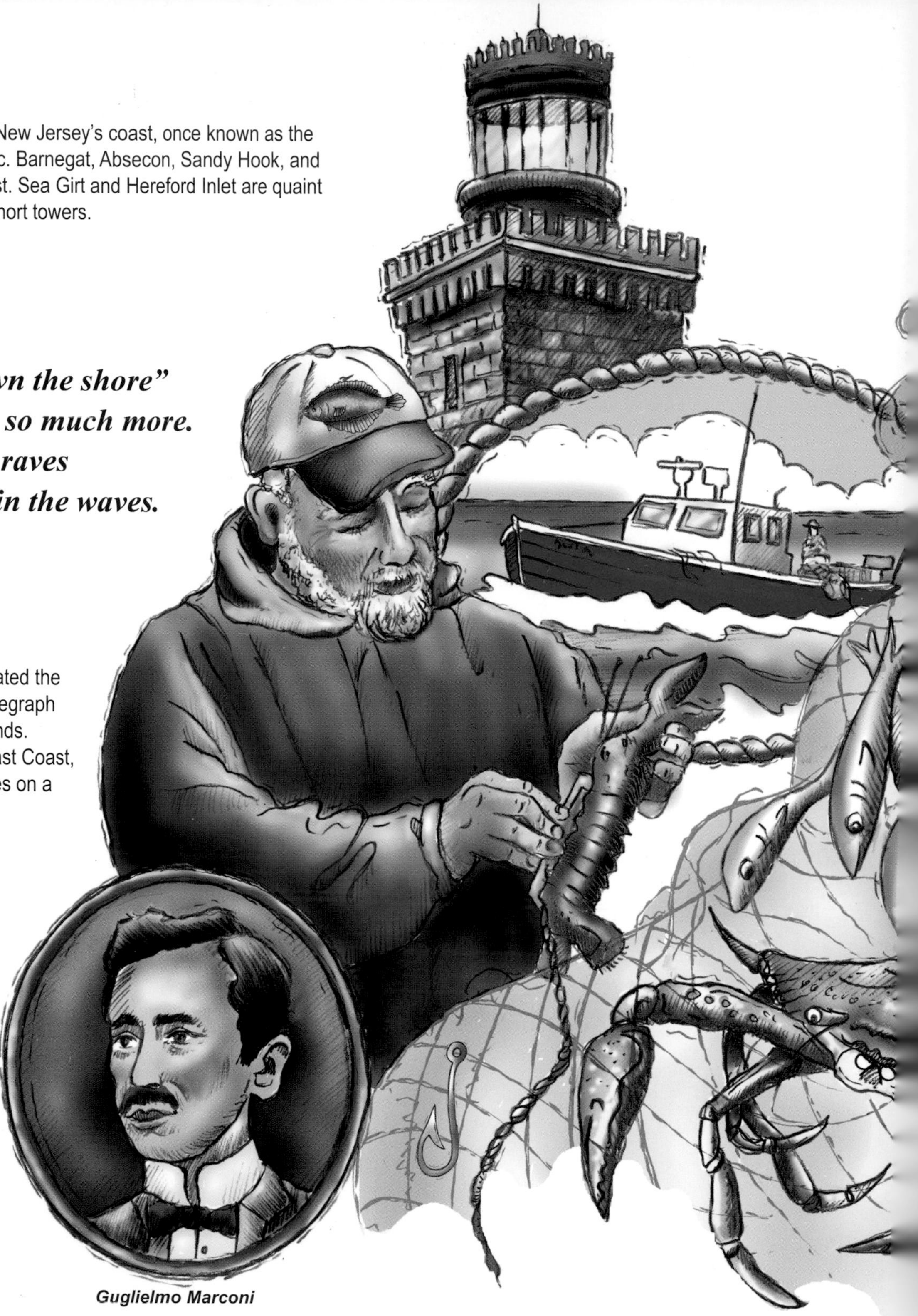

Guglielmo Marconi

Our fishermen harvest more surf clams and ocean quahogs than any other state.

Search for...

Clamshell

Squid

Absecon Lighthouse

Fishing hook

Fluke

Rising over 200 ft above the Atlantic Ocean, the Twin Lights of the Navesink have stood guard over the entrance of New York Harbor since 1828. The two towers are not identical twins; the south tower is square and the north is octagonal.

Meet a penguin up close and personal! You'll be amazed by the seals, sharks, and alligators at Jenkinson's Aquarium on the boardwalk in Point Pleasant Beach.

New Jersey fishermen catch over 75 million lb of seafood every year including lobsters, scallops, striped bass, bluefish, blue crab, menhaden, mackerel, fluke, weakfish (weighing up to 10 lb), monkfish, tuna, and squid (calamari).

Remember, in New Jersey, we don't just go to the beach; we go "down the shore."

Take your parents to Howell Living History Farm and feed the lambs, collect maple sap, harvest ice, make cider, and weigh the pigs.

Go white-water rafting.
Canoe the Delaware.
Hike through the water gap,
but watch out for the bear.

Still standing along the Old Mine Road is the Van Campen Inn, a "yaugh house." In the 1600s and 1700s this meant that, by law, the residents had to give shelter to travelers.

Take a drive along the Old Mine Road, one of the oldest roads in the U.S. Built by the Dutch in the 1600s, it once stretched all the way to Kingston on the Hudson River.

 Search for...

Puppet

Maple leaf

Calf

Shoe

Juggler's club

Fisherman

What is the Delaware Water Gap? It's a wide opening in the Kittatinny Ridge. Erosion has worn down the rock, and uplifting has raised the mountains. Even if your eyes can't see it happening, the gap is growing just a bit wider and deeper every minute.

In July, visit Frenchtown for the Bastille Day celebration with carriage rides, jugglers, mimes, magicians, and puppet shows.

Even in this most densely populated state, black bears still roam the woods. Sometimes they wander into towns, looking for food. If you see one, back away slowly. Do not run and never feed the bears.

Go to Lambertville in April for Shad Fest: try a shad fish sandwich and watch the fishermen haul in their catch from the Delaware River.

Sit under the 350-year-old Shoe Tree in Belvidere, as barefoot country folk once did while putting on their shoes before going to church.

Each May, thousands of Red Knots and other shore birds, flying from South America to Canada, depend on the horseshoe crab eggs for food. New Jersey is their first stop, so they spend up to two weeks chomping down thousands of eggs.

Hungry birds have flown a long, long way from way down south to the Delaware Bay. They carefully land on their spindly legs to chow down thousands of horseshoe crab eggs.

Mosey on down to Woodstown for the Cowtown Rodeo, over fifty years of calfroping, Brahma bull-riding, bronco-riding, steer-wrestling, and barrel-racing. It's the oldest rodeo on the East Coast.

Vineland is the largest city in area in the state—68.69 square miles!

Search for...

Horseshoe crab egg

East Point Lighthouse (since 1849)

Horseshoe crab

Eel

Teapot

The *A.J. Meerwald*, a 1928 oyster schooner, is a sailing classroom restored by the Bayshore Discovery Project.

In December 1774, during the American Revolution, New Jersey had its own tea party. Patriots in Greenwich burned a load of tea from the *Greyhound*, a British ship.

Horseshoe crabs have been on earth for 540 million years, since long before the dinosaurs. Every spring they come ashore along the Delaware Bay to lay their eggs in a shallow hole.

The *Maurice* (pronounced "Morris") River is one of the cleanest rivers on the Atlantic coast. It supports commercial crabbing, eeling, net fishing, and oystering.

Shellpile and Bivalve, on the Maurice River, remind us of the oysters harvested along the Delaware Bay. And yes, Shellpile does have a huge pile of shells.

Green Mountains

The state fair is here.
It's a ten-day delight.
There's so much good food
you'll enjoy every bite.

Hike in the mountains,
fish in the streams.
Northwestern New Jersey
is the land of your dreams.

Get your fill of cotton candy and slamburgers at the New Jersey State Fair. It's held in August in Augusta! Check out the tractors, taste that Jersey-fresh corn, and cheer on your favorite pig in the pig races.

At the Peters Valley Craft Center, learn photography, blacksmithing, silversmithing, woodworking, spinning, weaving, marionette making, and much more from professional artisans.

Search for...

Sailboat

Corndog

Water bottle

Hiking boots

Snowflake

Vacation at our mountain lakes for a fun-filled summer of boating, swimming, or just relaxing.

Climb the 292 steps of the High Point Monument to reach the highest point in New Jersey. What three states can you see?

Drive along the Old Mine Road, one of the first commercial roads in the US. Built by the Dutch in the 1600s, the road follows the Delaware River. It once stretched 104 miles to the Dutch settlements in Kingston, NY, on the Hudson River.

Explore Ringwood Manor, where colonial ironmasters forged a huge chain to prevent British ships from sailing north on the Hudson River. Each link was two feet long and weighed 114 lb.

Our Kittatinny Mountains are part of the long Appalachian chain that ranges from Maine to Georgia. Grab your hiking boots and backpack to explore New Jersey's 74 miles of the Appalachian Trail.

Slide down the slopes in Sussex County. If they don't have snow, they will make it. You can also cross-country ski at many of our state parks.

See the sharks and penguins and humorous hippos.
You'll giggle with chills from your head to your toes.
Be wowed by a dinosaur cousin of T-Rex,
or visit the battleship and play on its decks.

Now the state dinosaur, *Hadrosaurus foulkii* was named for Mr. Foulke and for the Greek words for large lizard. The bones show that the dinosaur was taller than a house and walked upright on two legs. Can you imagine!?!

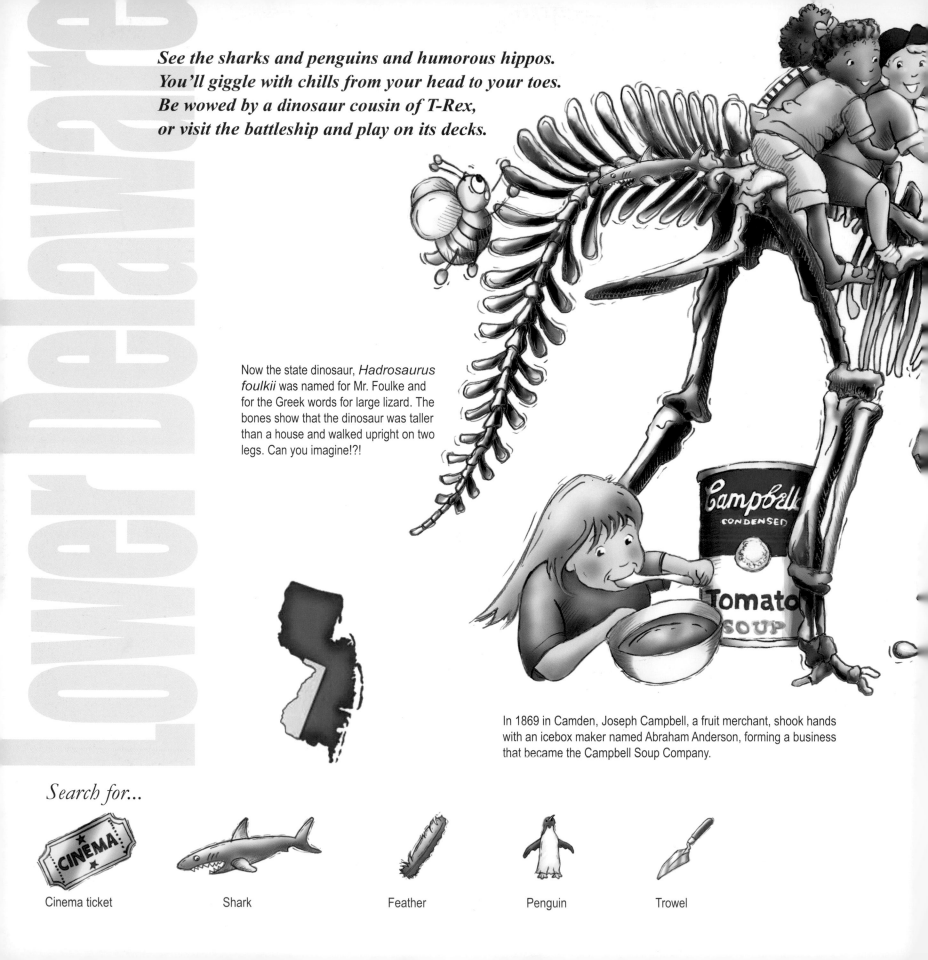

In 1869 in Camden, Joseph Campbell, a fruit merchant, shook hands with an icebox maker named Abraham Anderson, forming a business that became the Campbell Soup Company.

Search for...

Cinema ticket Shark Feather Penguin Trowel

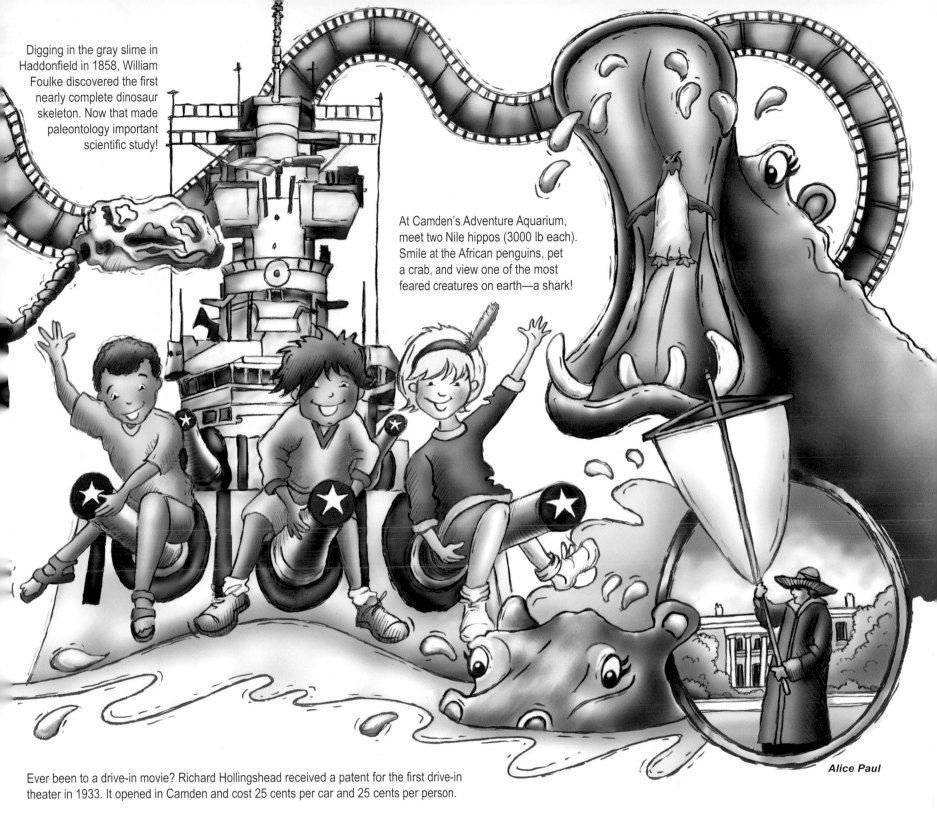

Digging in the gray slime in Haddonfield in 1858, William Foulke discovered the first nearly complete dinosaur skeleton. Now that made paleontology important scientific study!

At Camden's Adventure Aquarium, meet two Nile hippos (3000 lb each). Smile at the African penguins, pet a crab, and view one of the most feared creatures on earth—a shark!

Alice Paul

Ever been to a drive-in movie? Richard Hollingshead received a patent for the first drive-in theater in 1933. It opened in Camden and cost 25 cents per car and 25 cents per person.

Camden is home to the *Battleship New Jersey.* Climb into the 16 in gun turret and learn how projectiles were loaded. You can even stay overnight on this famous ship and stretch out on the bunks where sailors slept!

In 1758 our state's last Lenape families moved to Brotherton, the first Indian reservation. Unhappy in their new home, most had moved to Oklahoma, Wisconsin, and Canada by 1802.

Thanks to Alice Paul, women won the right to vote in 1920. This Mt. Laurel woman led picketers at the White House and wrote the Equal Rights Amendment. Visit her home, Paulsdale, to learn more.

The smell of chocolate is in the air at Hackettstown's Mars, makers of Three Musketeers®, Milky Way®, Starburst®, and delectable, delicious M&Ms®.

The Nabisco plant produces Ritz Crackers®, Oreos®, and Barnum Animal Crackers®.

The Lenape (Len-AH-pay), the earliest residents, had three clans: the Turtle, the Turkey, and the Wolf. The name Lenape means "ordinary people." Visit a recreated longhouse at Waterloo Village.

Lakes and mines in the Highland hills,
search for minerals and test your skills.

Ride in a boat in a car up a track,
snorkel and ski with a great candy snack.

Sussex County has 142 dragonfly species, more than any other county in North America!

Lake Hopatcong, our largest lake, is eight miles long. It was created to supply water to the Morris Canal.

Samuel Morse

Search for...

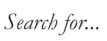

Trout

Dragonfly

Turkey

Hammer

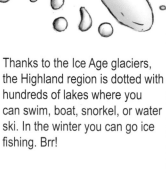
Thanks to the Ice Age glaciers, the Highland region is dotted with hundreds of lakes where you can swim, boat, snorkel, or water ski. In the winter you can go ice fishing. Brr!

Boats going uphill on dry land? Yes, the mountain-climbing Morris Canal crossed the Highlands using inclined planes. Boats in cradle cars traveled up and down on tracks between watered sections of the canal. Learn more at the Canal Society Museum in Waterloo Village.

Starburst

3Mu

MilkyWay

Zincite, willemite, and franklinite, mined nowhere else on earth, are just three of the 340 minerals found only in New Jersey. That's a world record!

Morristown is home to the Seeing Eye, North America's first school for training guide dogs for the blind. Look around town and you may see the instructors working with the dogs and their blind companions.

Listen to the howling of the wolves at Lakota Wolf Preserve, where you'll see tundra, timber, and Arctic wolves up close in a natural setting.

Bring your hammer to discover new minerals at the Franklin Mineral Museum, the fluorescent mineral capital of the world.

Think Samuel Morse invented the telegraph? Not exactly. Morse got the patent, but Alfred Vail did most of the work. Visit Vail's home at Speedwell in Morristown and find out what really happened.

Pine Barrens

Fort Dix has trained soldiers ever since it was built during World War I. Men and women from Fort Dix have served all over the world.

Spend a day at Tuckerton Seaport. Talk with decoy carvers, boat builders, basket makers, and fishermen and then climb to the top of the Tucker's Island lighthouse.

Driving down the Parkway, you'll see miles and miles of pines as you're passing through the Barrens where the sun most always shines.

In 1928, Mexican aviator Emilio Carranza, inspired by Charles Lindbergh, tried to fly nonstop from New York to Mexico City. On July 12, he crashed in the Pine Barrens during a thunderstorm. A monument was placed there in his honor.

Emilio Carranza

US ARMY FORT DIX

In the Brendan Byrne State Forest keep your eyes peeled for the insect-eating pitcher plants. They're very unique!

Search for...

Pitcher plant

Crucible

Airplane

Blueberry basket

Snowy owl

Red fox

Where will you find place-names like Double Trouble, Ong's Hat, Mount Misery, Red Lion, and Penny Pot? In the Pine Barrens, of course.

The Jersey Devil, a legendary creature, has haunted the Pine Barrens for over 250 years. People say he has a horse's head, wings, hoofed feet, and a piercing scream. Do you believe?

Listen to the toe-tapping music of the Pine Barrens every Saturday night at Albert Hall in Waretown.

The Woodford Cedar Run Wildlife Refuge in Medford helps injured animals, including the snowy owl, bald eagle, and grey fox.

If you dare, ride Kingda Ka at Great Adventure, the tallest (456 ft), fastest (128 mph in 3.3 seconds) roller coaster on earth. Too scary? Then try El Toro, the wooden coaster with a 76° first drop.

The Whitesbog Annual Blueberry Festival celebrates New Jersey's state fruit.

Can you imagine a horse diving into a pool forty ft below? During the 1900s in Atlantic City, you could have watched the girl on the high-diving horse as she led the horse up a long ramp and made a spectacular leap into a tank of water far below.

In New Jersey the people go "down the shore"
for beaches and boating and so much more.
Miles of coastline get all the raves,
as you play in the sand and swim in the waves.

Did you know that the properties in MONOPOLY® are named for streets in Atlantic City? The game changed many times, but in 1935 Charles Darrow became a millionaire when he sold his version to Parker Brothers.

CRAZ

MONOPOLY

Search for...

Herring gull

Teddy bear

Harbor seal

Saltwater taffy

Marble

Climb to the top of our eight lighthouses along the shore. Most are tall cylinders, but some look like houses.

Would you be surprised to see a 65-foot-tall elephant on the beach? Meet Lucy, the Margate Elephant! Climb the steps in her leg and look out through her eyes at the Atlantic Ocean.

Join the National Marbles Tournament on the beach in Wildwood in June. Only 7- to 14-year-old "mibsters" (marbleshooters) can compete.

Saltwater taffy was invented in Atlantic City when, according to legend, waves flooded the shop of candy maker David Bradley, soaking his supply of taffy. He later joked that now it is "saltwater taffy."

Tour Fisherman's Wharf, take a boat to see the lighthouses, or have a teddy bear tea party in Cape May, one of the country's oldest seaside resorts.

Why was the boardwalk invented? The answer is SAND! It was everywhere: in hotels, trains, and restaurants. Two men dreamed up a ten-foot wide wooden walkway. The sand on your feet would fall between the planks and back onto the beach, a clever idea that still works today!

The Marine Mammal Stranding Center in Brigantine has helped over 3000 stranded dolphins, seals, and sea turtles that washed ashore on New Jersey beaches. They've even helped a 25-ton humpback whale! Wow!

The Hook is home to a number of threatened and endangered species including the Piping Plover (a bird) and wild wormwood (a shrub). Check out the beach plums and prickly pear cactus, and keep your eyes peeled for red foxes, ospreys, horseshoe crabs, and monarch butterflies.

Wander around the buildings of Fort Hancock – the long row of officers' homes faces west with beautiful views of Sandy Hook Bay. Fort Hancock defended New York Harbor from 1895 until 1974.

Sandy Hook's location in the Atlantic Flyway gives birders many chances to view some of the 300 species that have been seen there.

The Hook is a sandy spit of land that juts out into the bay.
The lighthouse looks over the Jersey coast protecting ships on their way.

Search for...

Binoculars

Fox

1000 watt bulb

Holly

Monarch butterfly

Sandy Hook Lighthouse is the oldest light in continuous use in the United States. When built, the light was about 500 ft from the tip of Sandy Hook. Today, due to the shifting sands, it stands about 1.5 miles from the end of the peninsula.

The lighthouse is equipped with a Fresnel lens lit by a 1000-watt bulb. It is visible 19 miles out to sea. Today the lighthouse and Fort Hancock are part of Gateway National Recreation Area.

The Mount Mitchill Scenic Overlook, 266 ft above sea level, offers visitors a panoramic view of Sandy Hook Bay, the Atlantic Ocean, the New York City skyline, Fort Hancock, and the Sandy Hook Lighthouse. Geologic forces created the uplift.

With seven miles of beaches you can make a sand castle at Sandy Hook, a long peninsula at the northern end of the seashore.

By 1894, Fort Hancock had the nation's first and only steam-powered "disappearing gun" battery. The guns, mounted on elevator platforms, rose through openings on the roof and fired ½-ton projectiles up to seven miles away.

Sandy Hook is a 2,044-acre peninsula at the northern end of the Jersey shore with seven miles of ocean beaches for all to enjoy! The 264-acre maritime forest has the greatest concentration of American holly on the East Coast. Some trees are over 170 years old!

When a prehistoric volcano erupted millions of years ago, the lava oozed south, creating the ridges of the Watchung Mountains.

Watchung is a Lenape word meaning high hills—a good name, since the mountains are 400-500 ft high.

The Watchungs are a pleasant mix of parks and homes and zoos. With a president's home and Edison's lab, there is much for you to choose.

In the Watchung Reservation, wander through the Deserted Village of Feltville, where David Felt made paper until 1860.

Eagle Rock Reservation, a 408-acre park on the crest of the First Watchung Ridge, got its name from the bald eagles that nest in its rocky cliffs.

Volunteer at the Raptor Trust, one of the best bird rehabilitation centers in the U.S. Its state-of-the art hospital helps injured and orphaned birds get well and return to the wild.

Search for...

Falcon

Baby Ruth bar

Fox

Paper

Deer

Phonograph

In 1827, Sam Patch, the "Yankee Leaper," jumped 70 ft from the top of the Great Falls in Paterson, just for the fun of it.

Sam Patch

Edwin "Buzz" Aldrin, the second man on the moon, grew up in Montclair.

Edwin 'Buzz' Aldrin

Grover Cleveland

Thomas Edison

The Great Swamp National Wildlife Refuge is home to birds, fox, deer, muskrat, turtles, fish, and frogs. At one time the Port Authority wanted to pave it over to make an airport. Luckily for the animals, that plan was cancelled.

Grover Cleveland is the only president born in New Jersey. He is the only president to serve two nonconsecutive terms. The Baby Ruth candy bar was named for his daughter.

Thomas Edison had two invention factories in New Jersey. Here he created movies, record players, the incandescent light bulb, talking dolls, and even an electric car. He also improved his phonograph and created motion pictures here.

In 1777, Washington's Continental Army camped in the Watchungs at Middlebrook in Bridgewater. For the first time, the soldiers raised the new 13-star flag that had been adopted by Congress.

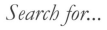
Gateway

Walk, jog, or bike along miles of walkways at Liberty State Park. The Statue of Liberty is so close, you can almost touch her. Hop aboard a ferry to visit Ellis Island and the Statue of Liberty.

See Lady Liberty, buses and bridges and ferries.
See tunnels and baseball and blossoms with cherries.

With rivers and cliffs and museums to see,
the Gateway of New Jersey's a great place to be!

Take a boat ride through the Meadowlands and you'll be amazed to see wetlands, turtles, shore birds, and grasses taller than you—just a few miles from New York City.

The cliffs of the Palisades tower hundreds of feet above the Hudson River—great for hiking!

Search for...

Baseball

Christmas tree

Turtle

Dock crane

Scout badge

In April, visit Branch Brook Park in Newark for the Cherry Blossom Festival. The park has more cherry trees than Washington, D.C.

The world's largest free-flying flag—the size of a basketball court—waves from the New Jersey tower of the George Washington Bridge on eight holidays.

When you take the ferry, check out the world's largest, free-standing timepiece – the Colgate Clock. Its octagonal face is 50 ft across. Now that's a big clock!

Explore Liberty Science Center, where you can operate a crane to unload ships or balance on a steel beam in the skyscraper exhibit.

The Rockefeller Center Christmas tree often comes from New Jersey. When the tree comes down in January, the trunk is given to the U.S. Equestrian Team in Gladstone for use as an obstacle jump for the horses.

Don't forget to stop in at the Newark Museum with so much to see and do. See how you can earn your scouting merit badge.

The first baseball game with modern rules was played on June 19, 1846, at Elysian Fields in Hoboken. The game's inventor, Alexander Cartwright, was the umpire; he fined one player six cents for cursing. (No, Abner Doubleday did not invent baseball in Cooperstown, NY.)

Why is New Jersey the Garden State? It's simple. New Jersey ranks in the top four in the production of cranberries, blueberries, bell peppers, and peaches.

Tomatoes, cranberries, strawberries, too.
Lettuce and squash and berries so blue.

Racing pigs and woolly sheep,
snakes that slither and chicks that peep.

Cows and goats, horses and hares,
see them all at the 4-H fairs.

Elizabeth White was the first person to successfully raise blueberries as a farm crop. Her team searched the swamps for the wild plants with the largest berries and planted them on the farm. Now the cultivated blueberry is the state fruit.

We have many animals on our farms, too. It's said that New Jersey has more horses per square mile than any other state. And they live in every county, even the most crowded ones.

Search for...

Farmer

Knife and fork

Lettuce

Chick

Diner

Pumpkin

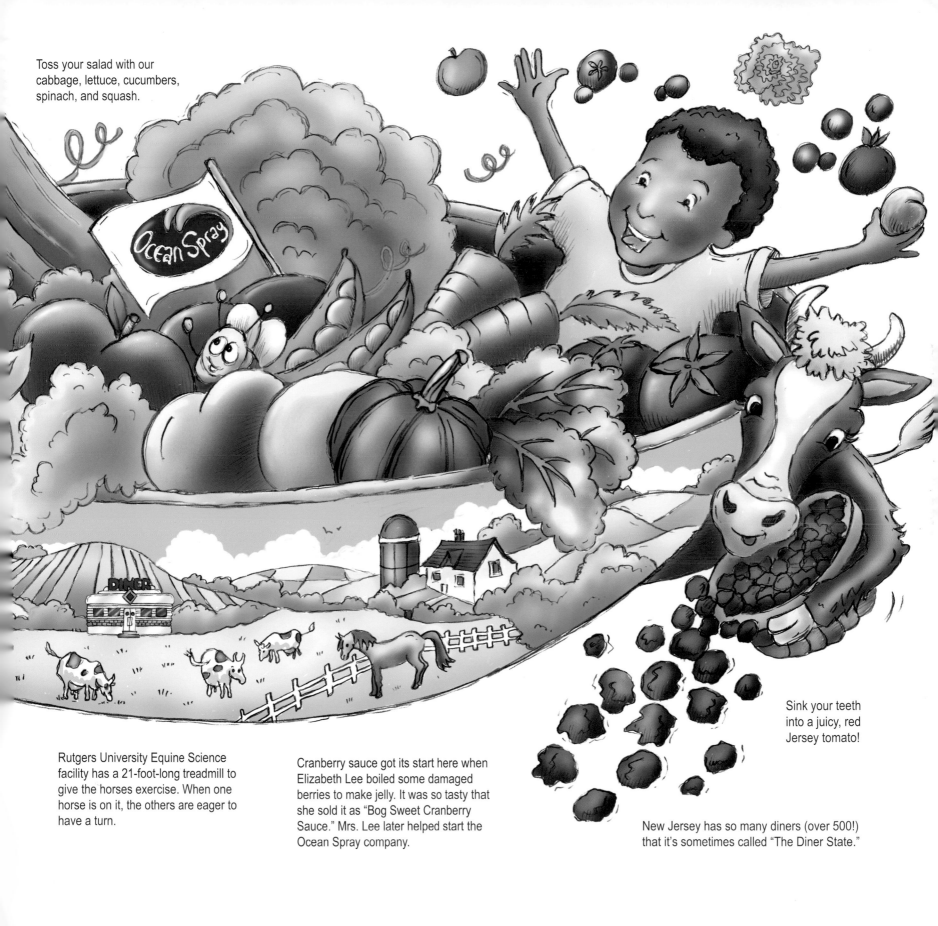

Toss your salad with our cabbage, lettuce, cucumbers, spinach, and squash.

Rutgers University Equine Science facility has a 21-foot-long treadmill to give the horses exercise. When one horse is on it, the others are eager to have a turn.

Cranberry sauce got its start here when Elizabeth Lee boiled some damaged berries to make jelly. It was so tasty that she sold it as "Bog Sweet Cranberry Sauce." Mrs. Lee later helped start the Ocean Spray company.

Sink your teeth into a juicy, red Jersey tomato!

New Jersey has so many diners (over 500!) that it's sometimes called "The Diner State."

To Marguerite Chandler, who inspired my love of New Jersey.
—*Linda J. Barth*

To Mike, NJ native, for supporting my work.
—*Hazel Mitchell*

Acknowledgements

With special thanks to the many people who shared their knowledge of the great state of New Jersey. We wish we had room to include all of your wonderful suggestions. Thanks for the gift of your time and enthusiasm.

Delaware Water Gap National Recreation Area; Alex Butrym, Barnegat Light State Park; Melissa Howard; Lynn Cooke, fourth grade teacher extraordinaire; Joyce Eagles, member, New Jersey Audubon Society; TroyJoshua, National Agricultural Statistics Services; Steve Coleman and Tony Ciavolella, the Port Authority of New York and New Jersey; Office of Legislative Services, State House, Trenton; Barbara Westergaard, Susan Poremba, and Robert Barth, my wonderful editors; Stacy Roth, History on the Hoof; Eric Olsen, Morristown National Historical Park; Essex County Park Commission; Jessie Havens, Somerset County historian; Ernest Bowers, Revolutionary War re-enactor; the students in Mrs. DeLorenzo and Ms. Francisco's 2006-07 fourth-grade class, Adamsville School, Bridgewater Township; the Ecological Research and Development Group, Lewes, Delaware; Shawn Viggiano and Paul Stern, Stokes State Forest; Tom Hoffman, Gateway National Recreation Area; Phoebe Hastings, Milltown School, Bridgewater; Daniel Dombroski, Geologist, New Jersey Geological Survey; Rod Kennedy, author of MONOPOLY: The Story Behind the World's Best-Selling Game; Vicki Gold Levi, author of Atlantic City: 125 Years of Ocean Madness; Atlantic City Historical Society; the staff of the Trailside Museum, Watchung Reservation; the staff of the Environmental Education Center, Somerset County Park Commission; the staff of High Point State Park; William J. Moss; Peters Valley Craft Center; Johnson & Johnson Company; the New Jersey Inventors Hall of Fame; Cowtown Rodeo; WheatonArts; the city of Vineland; the Bayshore Discovery Project; Palisades Interstate Park Commission; New Jersey Meadowlands Commission; Liberty Science Center; Rockefeller Center; the Alice Paul Institute; Doug McCray, the Battleship New Jersey Museum and Memorial; Adventure Aquarium; Campbell Soup Company; Lucy the Margate Elephant; Jenkinson's Aquarium; National Marbles Tournament; Tri-State Basset Hound Rescue; Marine Mammal Stranding Center; Capt. Bill McKelvey; Jo-Ann Liptak; Passaic County Parks Department; David Soo, Paterson Friends of Great Falls; Kenneth J. House; Karyn Malinowski, Rutgers Equine Science Center; Susan Finn and John Kraft, Lenape Lifeways; Joseph J. Myers, Aquaculture Development Specialist, NJ Department of Agriculture; the students in Mrs. Hatcher and Mrs. Kuker's 2006-07 fourth-grade class, Crim School, Bridgewater Township; Patricia Butler and Rebecca Creswell, librarians, Bridgewater-Raritan Regional School District; Roberta Rodimer, Walpack Historical Society; Customer Service, Ocean Spray; Joy Ricker, liaison for New Jersey Dairy Princess Committee; Kelly Mumber, librarian, Adamsville School, Bridgewater Township.

You can learn more great facts about New Jersey by visiting **www.VisitNJ.org and www.CelebrateNJ.org**.

MONOPOLY® is the registered trademark of Parker Brothers for its real estate trading game.
BAND-AID® is the registered trademark of Johnson & Johnson.
M&M®, Snickers®, and Milky Way®, are registered trademarks of Mars, Incorporated.
Baby Ruth® is the registered trademark of Nestle USA.
Tomato Campbell Soup® is the registered trademark of Campbell Soup Company.
Ocean Spray® is the registered trademark of Ocean Spray Cranberries, Inc.

Hidden New Jersey

Text Copyright © 2012 Linda J. Barth
Illustration Copyright © 2012 Hazel Mitchell

A Mackinac Island Book
Published by Charlesbridge
85 Main Street
Watertown, MA 02472
(617) 926-0329
www.charlesbridge.com

Library of Congress Cataloging-in-Publication Data on file

Summary: *Hidden New Jersey* is a fun seek and search book that will share the great state of New Jersey and teach new and interesting facts.

Fiction
ISBN 978-1-934133-23-1 (hardcover)
ISBN 978-1-934133-40-8 (paperback)

Printed September 2011 by Imago in Singapore.
(hc) 10 9 8 7 6 5 4 3 2 1
(sc) 10 9 8 7 6 5 4 3 2 1